INSTRUCTION MANUAL

Subject: Woman

101 Ways To Cherish A Woman

INSTRUCTION MANUAL

Subject: Woman

101 Ways To Cherish A Woman

ASHLY KOHLY

LEGACY Publishing Services
602 N. Wymore Rd., Winter Park, FL 32789
www.LegacyPublishingServices.com

Published by:
LEGACY Publishing Services, Inc.
602 N. Wymore Road
Winter Park, Florida 32789
LegacyPublishingServices.com

Copyright © 2007 by Ashly Kohly
ISBN 978-1-934449-01-1
Cover design by Gabriel H. Vaughn

For comments to the author, scheduling interviews or speaking engagements, contact through the *authors'* page at www.LegacyPublishingServices.com.

Printed in United States of America

All rights reserved. Written permission must be secured from the publisher to use or reproduce any part of this book, except for brief critical reviews or articles.

Dedication

This book is for real men that want ALL the real answers to women's everyday needs.

Foreword

To be a prince and a princess, one must first understand the fundamental emotions of elevating and nurturing the one they love.

The one emotional need that <u>drives a man</u> above all others is to be **admired**.

The one emotional need that <u>a woman desires</u> above all others is to be **cherished**.

Mr. Prince, this book will show you the simplest yet most profound ways to keep the fundamentals of your romance, love, and courtship vibrant for a happier, more stimulating relationship.

Use these simple, everyday suggestions to elevate your relationship to a whole new level.

Preface

If you have dated two times, two years or just celebrated your twentieth anniversary, this book is for you! Challenge yourself by doing even just one page of this book and your relationship will go to a whole new level.

Awaken your inner child and your inner wisdom, and be the strong, adoring man she longs to admire.

1

To Know Comfort

Sit your princess down, gaze into
her eyes, and as you sweep her hair
from her face say,
"You are so beautiful to me.
Every time I look at you,
I cherish you more and more..."

Expectation

She will feel safe and vulnerable like a
little girl and melt into your arms.

2

Timeless Class

Stand when she leaves or returns to the dinner table.

Expectation

You will be breathlessly admired.

Pampering

Rub her feet with heart-felt hands for five minutes or more.

She will sense your selflessness and want to please you in return.

4

Traditional Courteously

Promptly open her door when entering or exiting a room.

Expectation

You will be sexy to her because she will feel wrapped in your masculinity.

Effort

After any deed small or large,
say "Thank you."
Say "Thank you" every time she gives,
gets, or offers you something.

Expectation

She will be encouraged to
continue pleasing you.

6

Body Sense

Don't ever criticize her body. Don't agree with her when she says she looks fat.

Expectation

She will be confident in herself and in you.

7

In Sync

Find out what she enjoys doing and do it for a day. Note: Women want to feel that you can relate to them and enjoy what they enjoy, even if it's for just a moment.

Expectation

This creates intimacy and friendship for which there is no match. It may also motivate her to learn some of the things you enjoy.

8

Public Courtesy

In public, always put her first in all that you do.

Expectation

This is refreshing and comforting, very appealing to the opposite sex.

Admiration

At some point in your relationship, let her know that she is as beautiful today as the day you first met her.

This makes her feel like the most precious woman in the world, thus giving her a desire to always be pretty for you.

Profanity

Don't use vulgarity in front of your lady. She won't be impressed.

Expectation

She will think you're refined and a gentlemen worthy of the best she has to offer.

Romantic Practices

When you see that she has
too many items to carry,
gently take them out of her hands
while walking by her side.

She will realize how thoughtful
and strong you are.

Prayer

Say a prayer together before bed.

Expectation

There is no greater intimacy for a woman than to think you are strong and humble enough to go before the God of the universe and let him lead you.

Before She Knows

Surprise her with a piece of jewelry
on an ordinary day.
Note: All women love jewelry
and if it's no special occasion,
there is no wrong choice.

You will be her hero. She will
feel loved and appreciated.

I Double Dare You

Paint her toe nails with her favorite polish.

Expectation

It will make her feel that you want to take care of every little part of her.

Sleeping Beauty

Let her see you gazing at her
with loving eyes as she awakes.
If this can't be done, tell her
the next day how seeing her
sleep made you smile,
because she looks like an angel.

She will feel safe and beautiful
because of you.

16

Phone Inspirations

Call her at least once a day to say something nice.

Expectation

This will help lift any challenge she may be facing.

17
Post A Note

Hand wash her car and leave
a little sweet note on the seat saying,
"Your chariot awaits you, my dear."

Expectation

It's hard to compare to kind gestures
of love; she'll feel compelled to do
something wonderful for you.

No Comparison

When you are with her, pretend you don't notice any other women.

Expectation

She will think you really value her above the rest and it will make all other men that cross her path seem invisible.

Common Etiquette

"Please," "Thank you" and "You are welcome" are the most classy and gracious expressions in any situation.

Nothing takes the place of timeless etiquette. When one continually remains respectful, it sets the tone for how a woman sees you.

20

Fragrance

Compliment her on her fragrance.

Expectation

She will feel great that you notice.

21

PDA
(Public Displays of Affection)

In public touch her, hold her, and kiss her. Comfort her often with an accepting smile and loving eyes.

A woman will glow with pride because she will feel you want everyone to know that she is the apple of your eye.

22

Shakespeare

Take dance lessons, learn to play an instrument or learn a song with her.

Expectation

You'll laugh, have fun and feel connected.

23

Pet Names

Say good morning, noting her cute pet name daily. Some popular choices are: Baby, sweetie, princess, darling, foxy...

Expectation

This sets the tone for a positive, loving day.

24

Serious Courtesy

Always put the toilet seat down.

Expectation

She won't fall in.

Mirror

Always compliment her on the clothes she wears. Even when she doesn't look perfect, find something good to say.

Women need to feel you continually find them attractive. When they feel this, they will strive to be even more attractive for you.

Unselfish

Rub her entire body for an hour without expecting anything in return.

Expectation

This is an incredible unselfish act. She will shower you in ways you only dream.

27

Morning Sunshine

Wake her up with breakfast in bed for no apparent reason. Even if you can't cook it, buy it. It's the thought that counts.

Expectation

She will be happy to love and nurture you in return.

28

Sing

Write and sing a love song to her, no matter how short or silly.

Expectation

She will definitely smile.

29
Foundation For Fun

Get involved with one of her favorite activities and invite her to be involved in one of yours.

Expectation

Time spent with one another enhances friendship, which is the platform for respect and intimacy at any stage in a relationship.

30

Kisses

Softly kiss her fifty times all over her face and neck.

Expectation

Giggles.

31

Adoring Eyes

Thoughts we think shine through our eyes. When looking at her, practice thinking good thoughts.

Expectation

She will sense your positive thoughts and have more self-worth while magically feeling appreciated.

32

Happy

Tell her she makes you the happiest man in the world!

Expectation

This is what most women strive to do, so in turn you will make her feel very validated.

33

Pretty Woman

Go shopping with her and enjoy yourself. Help her pick out outfits to try on. Whatever you do, don't stand outside the store, it will embarrass her.

Expectation

She will feel like a Cinderella and you will be a prince in her eyes.

34

Butterfly

Tell her, "I love just watching you be you."

Expectation

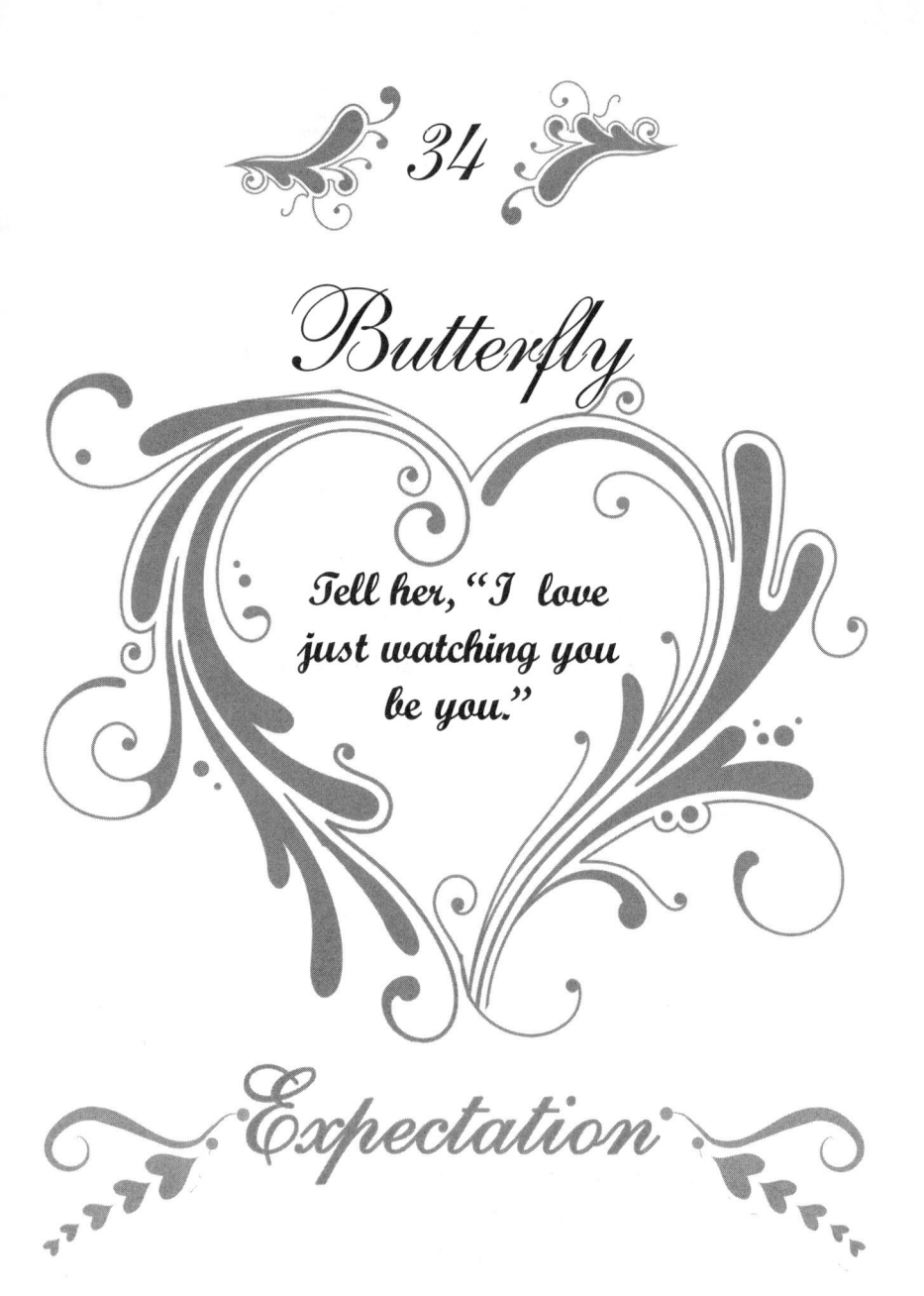

She won't need to have so much validation.

35

Kind Words

Uplift, encourage and re-enforce instead of criticizing and complaining. Note: Women are structured to receive and respond to positive emotions, which can be healing and nurturing.

Expectation

Kind words are uplifting, critical words are disheartening.

36

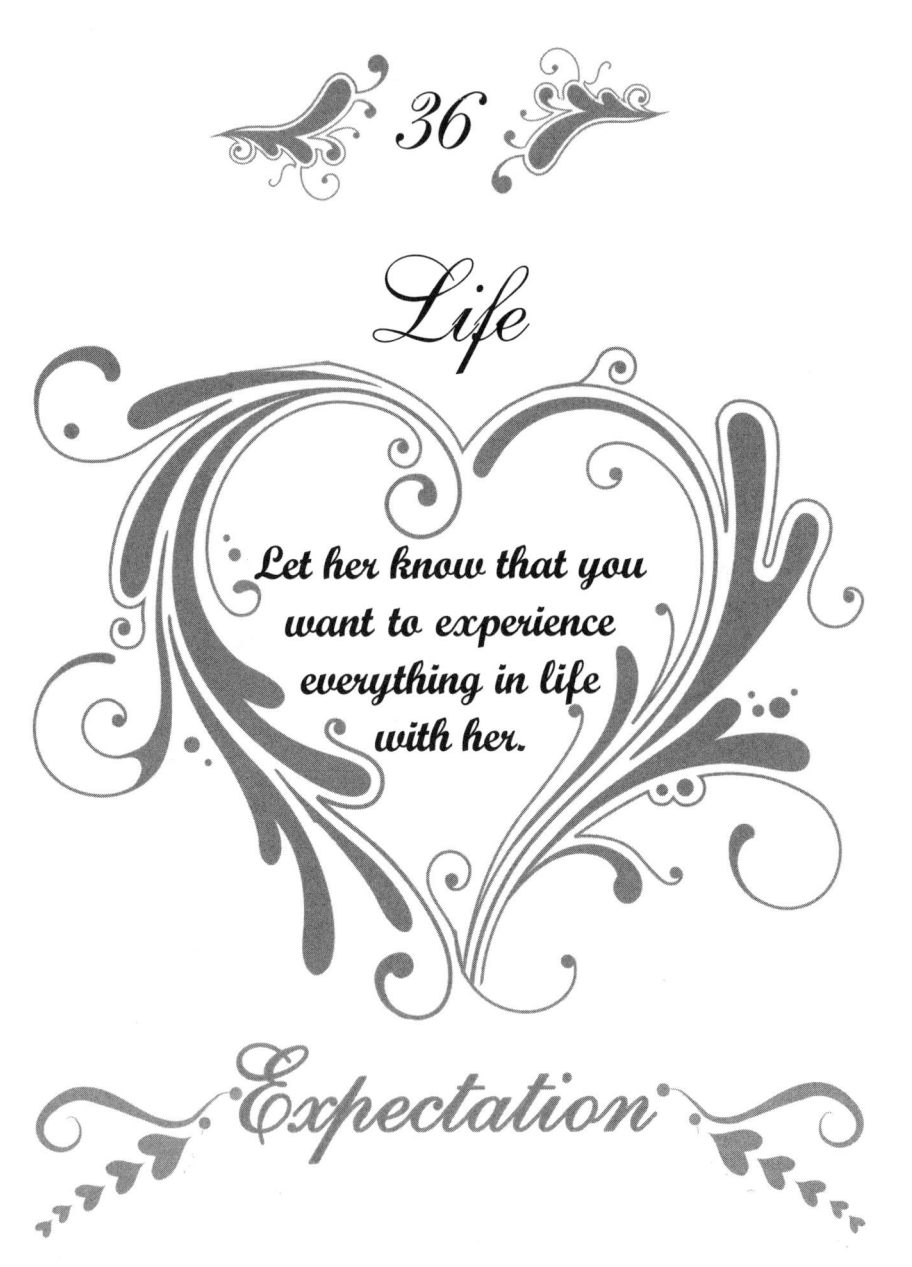

Life

Let her know that you want to experience everything in life with her.

Expectation

It will make her want to experience everything with you too.

37

The Queen

When in mixed company, focus on her. Let her know she's number one to you by touching or putting your hand on her back, arm, hips, etc.

Expectation

She will not question that she is the most important one for you.

38

Praise

When you see good, acknowledge it.

Expectation

Grass grows where you water it...

39

Wisdom

Listen without feeling the need to make a "fix it" comment or interjecting judgment. Look, nod and smile. Occasionally, women just need someone to listen.

Expectation

She will think you are wise.

40

Smile

Tell her, "I love watching you smile and laugh."

Expectation

She will want to smile and laugh around you more.

41

Know Her

Memorize her favorite color, animal, flower, perfume, time of day, diamond shape, flavor of ice cream, food and vacation spot.

Expectation

It shows you pay attention and she will really feel like you know who she is.

42

Dedication

Let her know you are dedicated to things that are good and true.

Expectation

She will honor you as a man with morals.

43

Natural

If you notice she's not wearing make-up, make it a point to compliment her on her radiant beauty.

Expectation

Women want to feel as if their man loves them they way God created them, which in turn makes them more comfortable with uninhibited expression of love for their mate.

44

Efforts

Whatever you want her to do for you, be prepared to do it for her.

Expectation

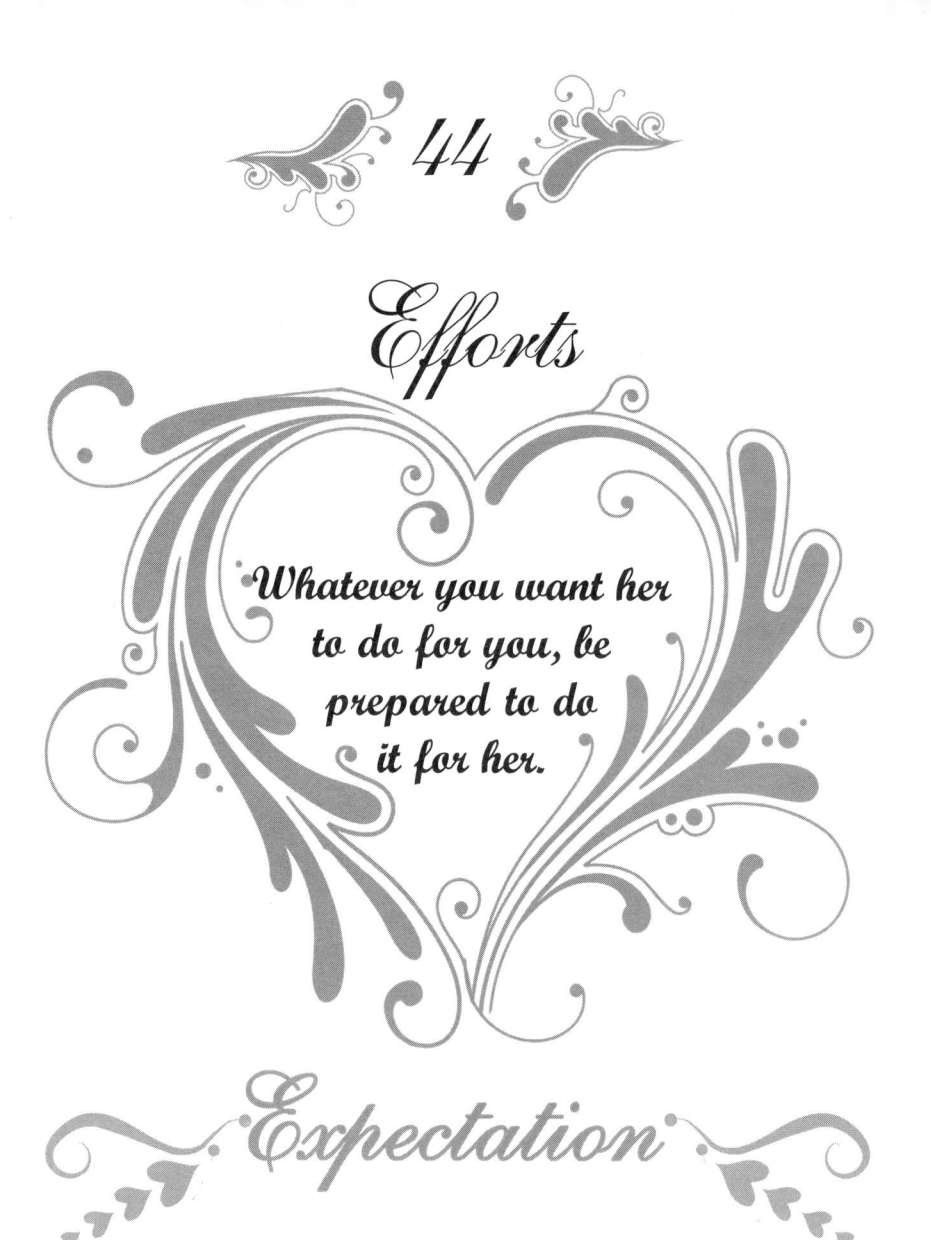

If a woman knows you would do the same for her as she would do for you — she will do so much more than you expect.

45

Style Choice

If she is being critical about the way she looks in an outfit, just tell her she looks slim or compliment her on the color and style.

Expectation

You will avoid an argument.

46

Spa Day

Give your woman a day of beauty.

Expectation

She will feel like a princess and think of ways to please you the whole time she is there.

47

Eye Contact

Look at her when she speaks, occasionally nodding and/or smiling when she makes a comment.

Expectation

One of the primary needs of a woman is to have respect from her man. When you look at her in the eyes and listen, it's a great sign of respect.

48

Story

Read her a bedtime story.

Expectation

It will be heart-warming and tend to her spirit and soul.

49

Unpredictable

Send flowers at least two times a year for no apparent reason, except to say how awesome, how appreciative, or how much you love her.

Expectation

She will experience an unexpected romantic gesture that lasts beyond the day.

50

Important

Let a woman know that her happiness means everything to you.

Expectation

She will look for ways to make you happy.

51

Romantic Recipe

- Sprinkle a pathway of flower petals leading to a warm bubble bath..
- lit candles
- glass of her favorite beverage
- soft music
- dim light
- Let her know all she has to do is relax.

Expectation

After a long day, if a woman is treated to this she will look out the window for your horse and chariot.

52

Light

Tell her, "Your eyes sparkle like stars."

Expectation

She will want to radiate in your eyes.

53

Her Hair

Ask her if you can brush her hair, then start from the bottom, gently and slowly work your way to the top.

Expectation

She will probably stop you and want to make out.

54

Women's Power

Say, "When I touch you I feel calm."

Expectation

As men are protectors, women are nurturers, so this will make her feel invaluable.

55

Gratitude

Give her a "Thank You" card for no apparent reason except to say, "I am grateful and thankful for you being in my life," or "Thank you for all that you do for me."

Expectation

It makes any hidden resentment go away and gives her a sense of self-worth.

56

Dreamy Float

Share an ice-cream float together and slip her an Eskimo kiss.

Expectation

She will think you are even sweeter than the ice-cream.

57

Promise

Make a her a deliberate promise to always tell the truth and that you will always put her first.

Expectation

She will exude a secure calm.

58

Togetherness

When speaking to her use the word "We" instead of "You" or "I."

Expectation

This will make her feel more secure in your relationship.

59

Insightful

Be gracious vs. being quick to grumble about what you do not like. Recognize her thoughtfulness, then state your preference.

Expectation

Since you've taken the time to recognize her sweetness, she will let you name your prize.

60

Poetry

Write from your heart, make it fun. Then, read your poem to her.

Expectation

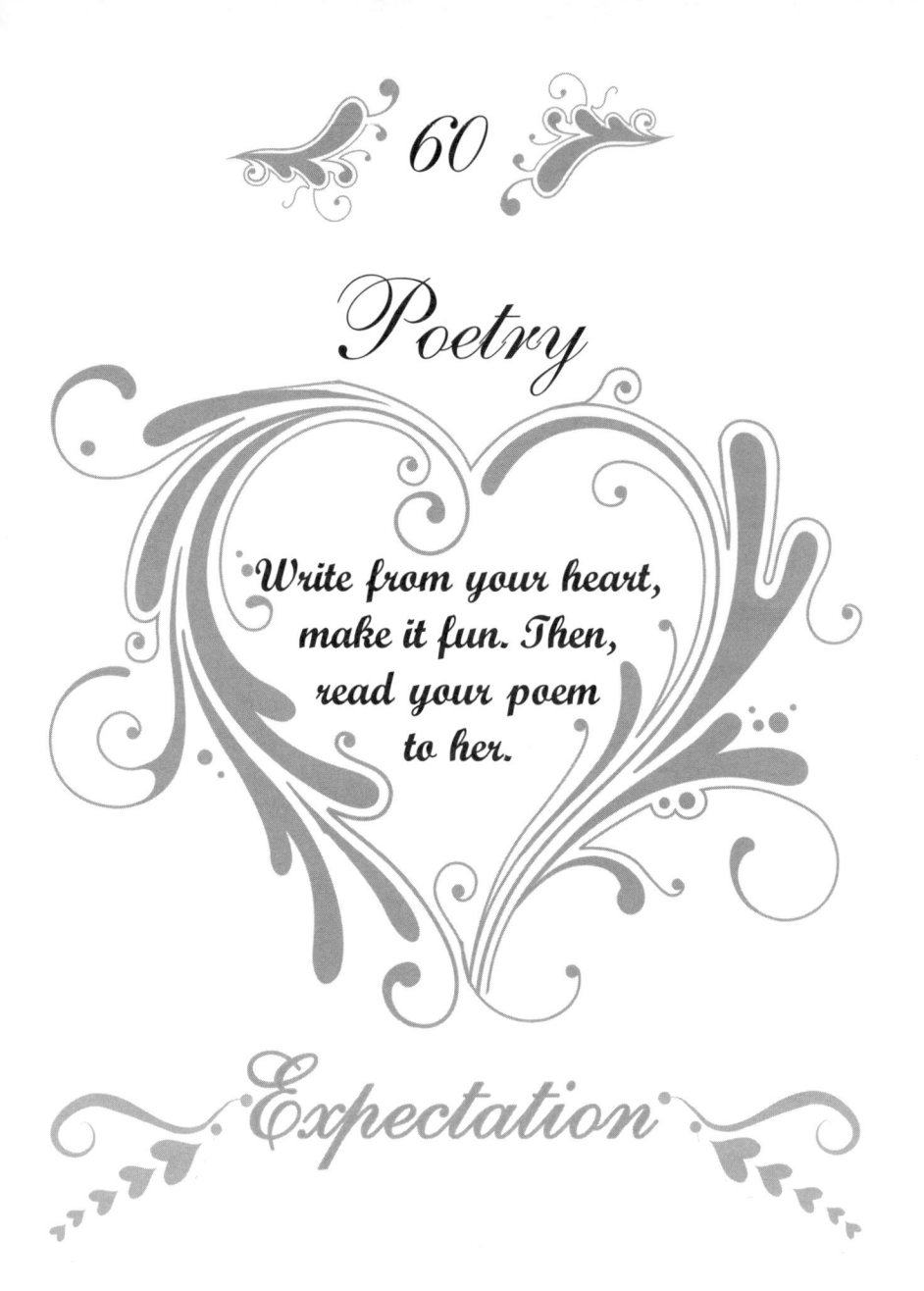

She will feel very flattered and adore you for this endearing act.

61

Pinnacle Of Respect

The greatest compliment in the world is to listen to her and let her know she is being heard.

Expectation

She will adore you, appreciate it and radiate confidence.

62

Dirty Work

Help her clean up
after a big mess.

Expectation

This comes across so
humble and thoughtful.

63

Face

As she is talking, smile and say, "I love listening to you talk and watching your facial expressions."

Expectation

She will feel confident in your presence.

64

Dreams

Ask her what her dreams in life are — and listen very carefully.

Expectation

She will feel as if you understand what she stands for.

65

Happy Heart

When she chooses to take her time and do something for the both of you, take a second to validate this by picking out one thing you recognize that's good about what she did.

Expectation

This will make her continue to be happy to do things for you.

66

Moods

Whenever she's feeling blue, compliment her.

Expectation

A kind word will lift her spirit.

67

Strolling

If she asks, "Why are you walking behind me?," tell her you love to watch her walk.

Expectation

She will put a pep in her step and a twist in her hips.

68

Laugh

When she laughs, let her know that it makes you smile.

Expectation

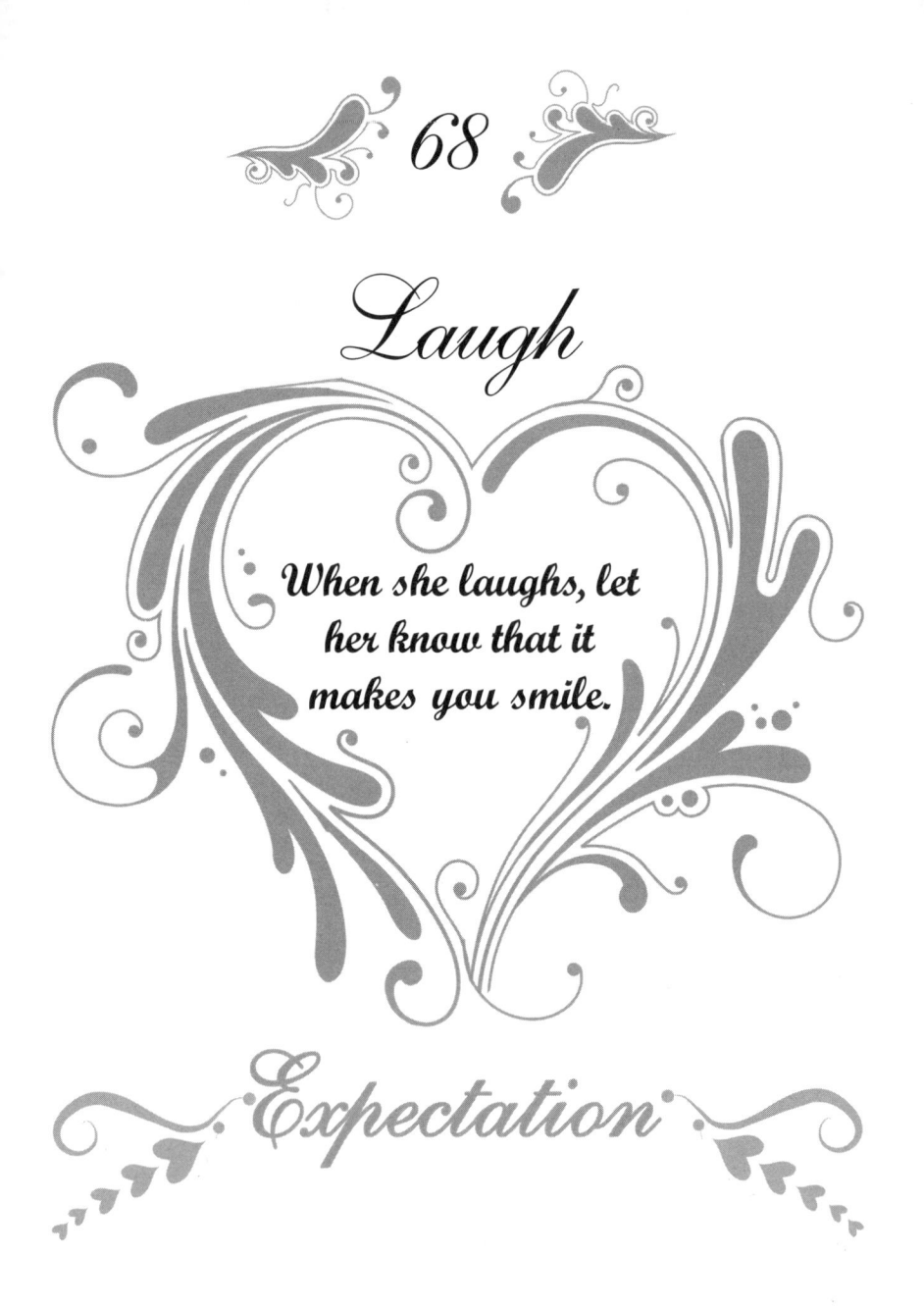

She will feel compatible with you.

69

Creation

Whenever she does anything creative such as decorate, draw, organize, cook, or think of a solution. Comment on how you think her creativity must come from heaven because she is so talented.

Expectation

She will try to make your world beautiful.

70

Hands

Hold her hand in public.

Expectation

This is timelessly appealing.

71

Sad

If she is faced with "big life stuff" that makes her feel sad, know that it's okay to be sad with her.

Expectation

You'll gain a best friend.

72

Faith

Show her you love her by trusting her with something you value.

Expectation

This will enlighten her world.

73

Your Thoughts

If she asks, "Honey what are you thinking?," either answer with, "I was just thinking how beautiful you are" or "I was thinking about what a great couple we make."

Expectation

Any other time that you are quiet, she will leave you alone with your thoughts, because she will assume you are thinking about her, even if you're not.

74

Fuel

Occasionally fill up her gas tank.

Expectation

She will feel that you care enough for her to give even when she's not in need.

75

Intimacy

As she lay, gently start at her head and run your fingers slowly over her nose, lips, neck, breast, belly button, hips, inner thigh and so on...
Do not let her move, only speak complimentary words.

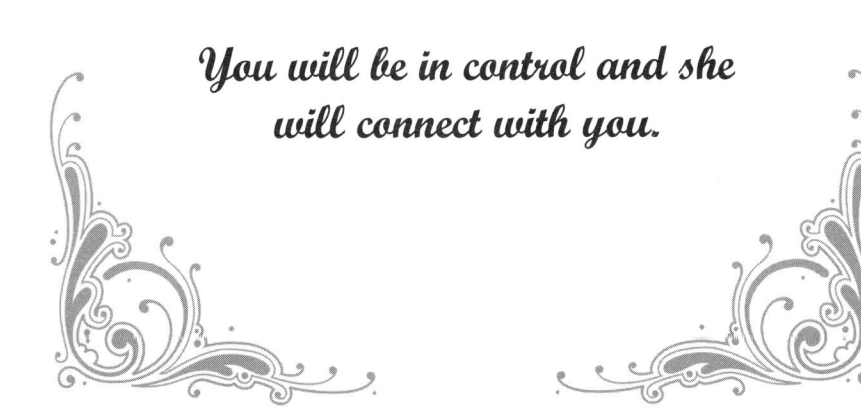

Expectation

You will be in control and she will connect with you.

76

Vote

Let her know you stand up for what you believe in.

Expectation

She will view you as a man who takes responsibility and that's attractive to any woman.

77

Masculinity

In all situations let her know you will do most of anything in the world to protect her.

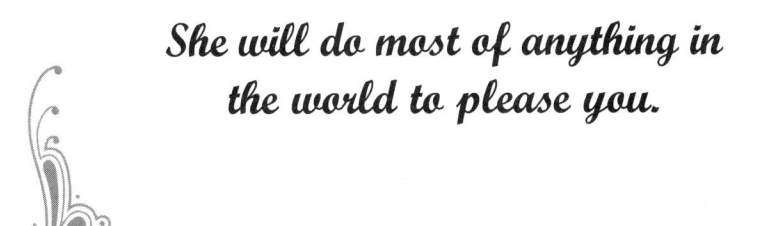

Expectation

She will do most of anything in the world to please you.

78

Excessive

Refrain from any behavior that appears excessively unhealthy.

Expectation

Great women stay with strong men.

79

It's All In The Fruits

Show her you love her by making healthy food choices and selecting foods that will appeal to your body, mind and vitality.

Expectation

You may inspire her to eat well while gaining her respect and admiration for taking care of yourself.

80

Self Aware

Dress nice. Take pride in yourself and surroundings.

Expectation

Her eyes will stay focused on you.

81

At Night

Cuddling is important to most women. Let her know that all you want to do is hold her in your arms all night long.

Expectation

Although she may not want to cuddle, she will think you really care about her.

82

Standing Tall

Let her overhear you praising her attributes to others.

Expectation

This will make her feel very special.

83

Thoughts

When you think good things be
sure to look at her.
Note: Love is the exchange of energy
— as you think so shall it be seen.

Expectation

Your eyes will radiate that she
is cherished and wrapped in your love.

84

Secret Fun

On your next date send her a drink from a secret admirer.

Expectation

She will feel sexy.

85

Angelic Spontaneity

Sand or snow, take your princess by the hand and make angels with her.

Expectation

This will be a vivid memory of fun.

86

Picnic

Have a picnic to celebrate life.

Expectation

You both will feel romantically refreshed.

87

Stay Cool

In any disagreement stay cool! Note: People tend to mirror one another in a conversation. So, act as you want her to act.

Expectation

Total respect, peace and calm will exude her.

88

Charity

Get involved in a charity together.

Expectation

This will bring you more intimacy than any other activity you can do together.

89

Expressions

Pay close attention to her facial expressions — they are a key indicator of how she is feeling.

Expectation

She will think you are so in tune with her.

90

Travel

When you are traveling, mail her a post card to let her know you are thinking of her.

Expectation

She will think you are romantic.

91

Cell Phone

When you are out together, refrain from openly consuming her time with your cell phone.

Expectation

She will feel that the time you spend together is valuable to you.

92

Creative Snuggling

Try not to use your hands while cuddling, you'll be surprised how creative you get.

Expectation

She will want to be as close to you as she possibly can.

93

Babies

Let her know you think she will make beautiful babies, even if she doesn't want children.

Expectation

She will feel amazing and attractive.

94

Thoughtful

When you are out call and ask her if there is anything she needs.

Expectation

She will feel important.

95

Generosity

Have something to give to a homeless person every time you encounter them.

Expectation

She will find you appealing for being compassionate to the less fortunate.

96

Taste Test

Put on light music, grab a blind fold and take turns playing "the food guessing game."

Expectation

This is a great stage-setter for innocence and trust.

97

Affectionately Speaking

Express affection without words. For example, put your arms around her and kiss her on the forehead.

Expectation

She will feel embraced.

98

Outside Romance

Plan a night outside with… a cd player, a bottle of her favorite beverage and a dance.

Expectation

She will be swept away under the stars.

99

Thoughtful Gift

Understand that a well-thought out gift can be more valuable to a woman than a last minute thoughtless one.

Expectation

She will appreciate that you sacrificed your time to plan for her.

100

Random Rose

In a public, random act of love offer her a rose just to say you think she is beautiful.

Expectation

She will feel like a pretty woman.

101

Ears

Nibble on the back of her ear.
Note: There are many nerve endings on the ear which can result in pure bliss.

Expectation

She will look for something on you to nibble.

About the Author

Ashly Kohly is a fourth generation author, born in Alexandria, Virginia. She is following a long standing tradition of sharing wisdom through authoring or public service. Ashly's great grandfather was an ambassador to Spain, her grandfather founded the New York Credit Exchange and pioneered innovative industries in Europe, and her father is a retired Holistic doctor. Dozens of books on medicine, business, politics and industry have been authored by the Kohly family. Ashly was voted in top five Celebration of Florida Authors at Barnes & Nobles. She has written and produced a TV show entitled, "The MOM Show." Ashly is a new mom, fitness instructor, and has produced several fitness videos. Ashly is an active professional speaker promoting the value of strong relationships between men and women. She is currently residing in central Florida with her husband, Greg, and their three year old son, Jacob.